World Religions General Editor: Raymond F. Trudgian

UNDERSTANDING YOUR MUSLIM NEIGHBOUR

MUHAMMAD IQBAL and
MARYAM K. IQBAL

LUTTERWORTH EDUCATIONAL
GUILDFORD, SURREY

First published 1976
Reprinted 1983

All references to the Holy Qur'an are from *The Holy Qur'an, Text, Translation, and Commentary*, Abdullah Yusuf Ali; McGregor and Werner, Inc., USA and to the *Hadith, Sahih Al-Bukhari — Arabic–English, Vol. II*, Dr. Muhammad Muhsin Khan; Islamic University, Al-Medina Al-Munawwara, Saudi Arabia, 1971.

ISBN **0 7188 1857 1**

Printed in Great Britain by
Fletcher & Son Ltd, Norwich

CONTENTS

LIST OF ILLUSTRATIONS

For permission to reproduce the above photographs, the Authors and Publishers are indebted to: Pakistan Embassy for numbers 1, 2, 4, Ibrahim Muhammad, General Secretary, Federation of Students Islamic Societies of UK and Eire for number 3, Bashir Ahmad, Secretary, Huddersfield Council of Islamic Affairs for numbers 5, 7, 10, 13, 16, Elizabeth M. Wilson for number 6, Peter Meal, Headmaster, Spring Grove County Primary School, Huddersfield for number 8, Elizabeth Hayes for number 9, Ashraf Ali for numbers 11, 12, 14, 15. Thanks are due to Frank Micklethwaite, Audio-Visual Adviser, and Elizabeth Hayes of the Audio-Visual Department, The Polytechnic, Huddersfield for all their help.

EDITOR'S INTRODUCTION

The response to our *Thinking About* series showed the need for basic foundation books which could be used by pupils in Junior and Middle Schools. The books in this *Understanding Your Neighbour* series present the festivals, places of worship and other customs of the various faiths now represented in this country.

The children who use these books will have reached what Jean Piaget, the educational psychologist, calls the 'concrete' stage of thinking. This is defined in *Religious Education in Primary Schools* (Schools Council Working Paper 44) as the stage where, 'the child now begins to be able to think more logically, to relate different aspects of a situation, to classify data, and to check over his thinking. He is still limited, however, to thinking mainly about specific objects . . .'

This research has been born in mind in the preparation of these books. It is now becoming accepted that World Religions can be dealt with at the Junior and Middle School level by introducing the specific festivals and customs of other people. Another accepted approach is through the use of themes such as 'light' and 'water', elements known to the pupil which recur in the practices of many religions.

The General Article introducing the Christian Education Movement Primary Resource material on 'Living in a Multi-Faith Society' agrees that this phenomenological approach is the way to study other faiths in the classroom but states that this method, 'Can easily degenerate into a "bits and pieces" method'. It goes on to say:

> Most religious beliefs and practices can be understood only in the context of the faith as a whole, and great care must be taken therefore to select only those examples which are not misleading when studied apart from that context . . . While pupils cannot be expected to see religion as a whole, teachers should not venture into the field of other faiths without the support of good resource material and without the willingness to study the religion seriously and gain some sort of overall understanding.

We have attempted to present this 'overall' picture in these books in such a way that not only the teacher but also the pupil can come to a balanced understanding of their neighbours' faith.

The specific and concrete examples of events, customs and buildings are presented in the context of the faith in order to help the pupil not only to acquire new facts but to perceive the experience of a child who lives in another culture.

Through the study of this series of books, pupils should be able to discover their own themes and to see the similarities and differences.

Again to quote from the CEM Primary Resource material:

> World Religions in Education is certainly not an attempt to gloss over differences, to pretend that all religions are really the same, but it does help pupils to see that the religious quest is common to mankind, that certain elements are found in most religions, e.g. worship, sacred places, sacred writing, beliefs about the significance of a man, a sense of the mystery of life, etc. even if the form may vary. The emphasis is on what unites men rather than on what divides them.

This is the emphasis of these books as they seek to lay a foundation of knowledge and appreciation in the Primary school to counteract the stereotype so prevalent in their environment which often prevents them from 'Understanding their Neighbour'.

Isleworth, Middlesex   Raymond F. Trudgian

A LETTER OF INTRODUCTION

Dear children,

Can you imagine pumping water for your pet buffalo, having lessons in the shade of a *pippal* tree or learning a foreign language at the age of six? Do you know where the *Ka'aba* is? What the *Holy Qur'an* and the *Hadith* have to tell?

This is a story about two children and their family. As the story unfolds and you get to know the characters, we hope you will learn something about the religion and customs of Islam, whose followers are called Muslims. Islam is not a religion for special occasions, it is a complete way of life, meaning submission to the will of Allah (God).

Although the characters in the story are not real, people like them do exist. They may, in fact, live very near to you.

Yours very sincerely,

Muhammad Iqbal &
Maryam Khanum Iqbal

Note: C.E. = Christian Era

THE OPENING

In the name of Allah the Beneficent, the Merciful
Praise be to Allah, Lord of the worlds,
The Beneficent, the Merciful.
Owner of the Day of Judgement,
Thee alone we worship,
Thee alone we ask for help.
Show us the straight path,
The path of those whom Thou hast favoured
Not the path of those who earn Thine Anger
Nor of those who go astray. (*The Qur'an* I:1—7)

Muhammad Bashir put his slate and chalk into his sister Shamim's bag as they set off for the village school. Their mother, Zamir Akhtar, watched them as they walked across the courtyard into the cobbled street. '*Khuda Hafiz* — may God take care of you' she called as she waved goodbye and returned to the kitchen where ten minutes before they had all been eating their breakfast. All, that is, except for her husband.

Abdul Haq often sent his family money and news of his new life in England. He had been there for two years now. When he had first gone to England he had only intended to stay for a short while so that he could earn money for himself and his family, including his parents, brothers and sisters and all close relatives. But now he seemed to like the idea of settling down in his new country.

Zamir, however, did not like the thought of leaving her hard but simple village life among her family and friends to go to a strange land. Her own mother had lived with her ever since her father had died. Her brother Yusuf lived across the courtyard. He had a small farm and spent most of his time in the fields. His wife Fatima helped him to look after the animals and sold vegetables and dairy products in their little greengrocer's shop.

Upstairs she could hear her mother puffing up the bed quilts. Each one had been covered in a beautifully embroidered cross-stitch pattern which Zamir had sewn in her spare time. It is the duty of a Muslim woman to look

1. A village woman.

after her home and family first and jobs were not available in the village. Zamir folded the prayer mats and put them on the chair ready for lunch-time prayers.

She and her mother prayed five times every day and the children went to the Muslim place of worship, the mosque, every morning before their breakfast. There they were taught *Arabic*, which is the language of the Muslim, the meaning of the Muslim's Holy Book (the *Qur'an*) and the *Hadith* or the sayings of the Prophet of Islam, Muhammad. They also heard stories about the Prophet and his followers and the great men of Islam.

Shamim and Bashir enjoyed the stories of kindness to animals. Among the sayings of Muhammad they had found some forbidding the use of animal skins for floor covering, and using animals for fighting and target practice, and the killing of she-goats, which gave milk.

Shamim's favourite story was that of Nasir-ud-Din, a king's servant, who later became the ruler of Afghanistan. One day when he was hunting he saw a baby deer. Thinking it would make a wonderful pet for his children, he caught it, put it on his horse and rode away. The mother deer soon dis-covered the loss of her dear fawn and panic-stricken, ran after the hunter. After a while Nasir realized that he was being followed and turned to see the deer approaching. As she drew near she looked up into his face and with her big sad eyes seemed to say to him, 'You have taken my baby, what do I care for my life now?'

Even the thought of his own children's pleasure at receiving the delight-ful pet could not stop the hunter from releasing the fawn. As the happy pair disappeared into the forest the mother turned to look back and Nasir felt she was saying a very big 'Thank you' to him. That night, the Prophet Muhammad came to him in a dream saying 'Allah will make you a king — but take care! As you took pity on that poor deer so you must be kind to all of Allah's human creatures also!'

He who kills even a sparrow needlessly is accountable to God on the Day of Judgement. (*The Hadith*)

LIGHTEN OUR DARKNESS

He who goes out in search of knowledge is in God's path till he returns. (*The Hadith*)

Shamim was ten. Bashir was only six and had not been going to school very long. They liked school especially now that the warm days had come.

11

They would have lessons on the verandah or outside in the shade of a large *pippal* tree.

As they reached the school the bell began to ring and they ran in. Work began with an assembly. Today Shamim was a little nervous for she would be leading the prayers with her friend Kausar. That was a great honour and she felt so proud. They had learnt a Song of Devotion by heart, and she was very anxious to get it right.

My desire to be a light-giving lamp finds its expression in my prayers
O Lord, let my life be a lamp.
And let the darkness of ignorance for ever be foreign to my mind
O Lord, let me be covered eternally by light.
Just as the garden wears its crown of flowers so let my country uphold me with pride
Let me, my Lord, blossom for ever and ever more.
A never-ending thirst for knowledge be mine
O Lord, give me the desire to pursue the light of knowledge to the end like the fluttering fireflies.
Let my life be dedicated to the cause of the poor, old and sick
O Lord, let me always be kind, loving and friendly to everyone.
And above all, always keep me away from evil thoughts
And guide me, Lord, for ever, along the pure and right path.
(Translated from an *Urdu* poem — A Child's Prayer)

At lunchtime the children filed out of school. It was very hot and they did not feel like running.

'There is grandmother,' yelled Bashir as he pointed to Shahida Begum, his grandmother who was chatting to some of the women at the well. They were lucky, they had their own small hand pump in the courtyard which the two families shared with Shahida Begum's brother and his family. As they walked home, Shamim enjoyed telling her grandmother about the service. She knew it would please her. She remembered how the old lady had told her all about her pilgrimage to Mecca last year.

Mecca is a very holy place for Muslims. Although they believe that God is everywhere and in everything, His special House of Worship on earth is in the *Ka'aba* at Mecca. This famous cube-shaped building is believed to have first been constructed by the Prophet Adam, later rebuilt by the Prophet Abraham and finally by the Prophet Muhammad.

Shamim wondered how grandmother had not got lost among the huge crowds while she was there, but the old lady had enjoyed the noise and bustle and also the endless muttering of the Holy Scriptures all around her. She had been well cared for by some other villagers who had made

2. School in the open-air, Parachinar.

3. The *Ka'aba* at Mecca.

the trip and many a kind stranger offered her a brotherly helping-hand. Shamim knew that one day she would go to Mecca to the *Ka'aba*, and the Black Stone. She thought she would enjoy throwing stones at Satan but she could not imagine her gentle grandmother throwing stones at anyone or anything at all.

'Did you sing well, Shamim?' Zamir smiled at her daughter, as they entered the kitchen.

'Yes,' replied Shamim who grinned broadly. 'Teacher said it was the best this year.'

'I got all my sums right,' boasted Bashir determined not to be outdone.

'Well done both of you!' exclaimed their mother, 'You deserve a surprise! Let's first do our jobs, have something to eat and then I'll read you some important news.'

While Shamim helped her mother prepare the meal, Bashir went into the yard to feed the chickens and give the buffalo some water from the hand pump. Shahida Begum curled up on the mat, took out, and began to toll, her prayer beads called rosary, '*Subhanallah* — glorified God, *Alhamdulillah* — praise be to God, *Allahu Akbar* — God is Great'. Thirty-three of each and an extra *Allahu Akbar* to make 100. She also took out a little leaflet containing parts of the Holy Qur'an and read it over and over

14

again.

Her father had been a 'Sufi', a very pious man who had lived and worked in the village and brought up a large family, yet he had found time to devote his life to God. Not for him the city life nor that of another land far away, only a simple home, the floor for his bed, collarless flowing shirt and long loin-cloth to cover him and a bowl of lentils to feed him. This had been his source of happiness; his work, his family and his constant prayers. There are many stories about great Muslim *sufis* — or mystics (both men and women) who, through their continuous prayers and devotion to God developed powers of understanding, healing and physical endurance beyond those of most normal men.

A DECISION IS MADE

The children ate their meal with unusual speed that day. When they had thanked God for their food they sat with their mother who took out an air mail letter. She opened it out carefully and the already excited children immediately recognized the Great Britain stamp and the familiar handwriting of their father:

My dear wife and loving children,

Assalamu Alaikum! — Peace be on you — I hope you, mother-in-law, brother and sister-in-law, Yusuf and Fatima, and nephews Ajmal and Zahir are all well. Greetings also to brother-in-law Ashraf and Farida and their children. I have written to my parents and brothers and sisters and they will come to see you soon no doubt, I hope so, as today I have made an important decision which will be for the good of our little family, may the blessing of Allah be upon us.

I have now bought the little house I told you about in my previous letters. Soon it will be decorated and furnished so that you and the two children may join me here.

The first thing to do now is to get passports for yourself and the children, then you will need the visas. After that my brother Imam-ud-Din will arrange for the air flight. You may have to wait a long time for the documents so do not worry or be upset. I am so much looking forward to seeing you and the dear children once more. Your brother will help you and you must listen to their advice. Blessings to you all. I will write again soon.

Your loving husband,
Abdul Haq.

'Hooray, hooray, we're going to England! We're going to see daddy,' the children chorused in excitement. Their mother folded the letter and looked across at her mother. Shahida Begum nodded her head thoughtfully then turned towards the children and smiled at the thought of their happiness at being united with their father.

'You must go as soon as possible,' she spoke softly and patted her daughter's hand. 'See how happy the children are and it will be better for you to be with Abdul once more. It is Allah's Will my child. We will talk over the arrangements with Yusuf. Ashraf is coming on Saturday. No need to worry. Everything will be all right.'

THINKING ABOUT MARRIAGE

'That was a delicious curry,' Ashraf remarked to Fatima and he emptied some water from the *lota* or metal jug and washed his hands. 'I should let Parveen and Shamim make the tea. The young ones can play in the courtyard,' he said, ushering her back to the main room where her husband and the rest of the family were sitting.

Shamim liked to help her cousin Parveen. Whenever she came to the village Shamim would follow her everywhere, watching every move and listening to every word. Today Parveen was wearing much tighter *shalwar* or trousers than usual.

'Are they new?' enquired Shamim.

'I made them yesterday with my dress,' confided Parveen. 'Father says they are too tight but all the girls in the towns and cities are wearing pyjamas now instead of the baggy *shalwar*.'

'Mummy says it is better to wear loose trousers,' Shamim replied.

'Have some *jalebi*.' Parveen offered her cousin a squiggly syrupy sweet. Shamim loved *jalebi* and accepted it gratefully. Shamim looked up at Parveen's smiling face. She thought her cousin had beautiful eyes. The black *surma* outline seemed to make them bigger and more sparkling than ever.

Now that Parveen was seventeen, Ashraf hoped that she would be married to his cousin's son next year. Parveen had left school last summer and helped by serving in his new shop. If she had been clever enough she could have gone to the University in Lahore to study to become a teacher or even a doctor, but it was not to be. She would be happy now to be married and have a family of her own to care for.

4. A bride wearing her dowry.

Already his daughter and her mother were saving materials and goods in preparation for her marriage. Marriage celebrations take place before and after the marriage ceremony depending upon the custom of the country or family, but the actual Muslim marriage is a very simple ceremony. Before witnesses, the couple repeat passages from the Holy Qur'an and each repeat their consent to the marriage three times. After the ceremony, the *Imam* or religious leader and guests pray for the couple. Sweets like small cakes and tea are provided and the service has ended after only a few minutes. It is the responsibility of both families to make sure that the couple remain happy together.

> The best of treasures is a good wife. She is pleasing to her husband's eyes, obedient to his word and watchful over his possessions in his absence, and the best of you are those who treat their wives best. (*The Hadith*)

PREPARING TO DEPART

In the weeks that followed, Zamir, having bought wool and cloth from the town, spent all her spare time knitting cardigans for herself and the children and making *shalwar* and dresses called *qameez* in heavier material which she felt would be suitable for a cold English climate.

The children had finished school for the summer holidays and were busily tending the vegetable patch where aubergines, onions, chillies, okra, and coriander were growing. Bashir looked after the cauliflowers and liked to measure them with the span of his hand and his fingers. He would squat and watch them carefully for what seemed like hours and was convinced that they had grown every time he measured them, even though hardly half a day had passed. Shamim helped her mother to pack. Many of the villagers had invited them to their homes for a meal and had given them gifts to distribute to their relatives in England. Zamir hoped that their luggage would not be overweight as she watched the steadily growing pile of goods.

Shamim's uncle Yusuf was very busy in the fields now that the rain had come. Their own crop was being tended by Mr Arshad and his sons who were employed in pulling out the weeds. Rain was good for them too! She wondered if it was raining in England.

'England, England' she repeated the name softly to herself and it seemed as if it would never leave her thoughts until she, Bashir and her mother were there with her father in their new home.

5. A market scene at Peshawar.

THE FAMILY UNITED

Among the believers who show most perfect faith are those who have the best disposition and are kindest to their families. (The Hadith)

When the plane arrived at Manchester Airport it seemed an eternity since Zamir and her children were saying their very last goodbyes to Imam-ud-Din and his family at Rawalpindi Airport. Their tear-stained faces had long since dried and now only the urgent longing to be united with husband and father was uppermost in their minds.

As they stepped warily on to the steps outside the plane they were met by a damp current of air which brought fresh tears to their eyes. The air hostess helped them off the steps and guided them into the Immigration Office.

After they had had their passports, visas and medical certificates checked, they took their baggage through the customs. As they moved out, a man of middle height, with thick black hair and a happy smile on his face, walked towards them.

'There's daddy,' Zamir pointed as she quickened her pace.

The two children ran towards him and he opened his arms to welcome them. Shamim felt her heart miss a beat as she ran into her father's arms.

'Oh daddy, daddy,' she sobbed as she felt the warmth of his hand against the cold of her cheeks. He was just the same as she had remembered him, a little thinner and paler perhaps, but this was her father and they were together at last. She felt as if it was all a dream as he hugged and kissed them both. Then he became aware of Zamir close behind him. They both smiled very happy smiles and greeted each other but neither touched the other, for it is not the custom for Muslim husbands and wives to embrace in public — not even on such a momentous occasion. But now the little family, united at last were on their way to a new home.

SETTLERS IN A STRANGE LAND

If you are mindful of God, He will be mindful of you, and if you are mindful of God you will find Him before you. When you ask for anything ask it from God, and if you seek help, seek help from Him. (*The Hadith*)

Number Nine Newcombe Street was in the middle of a small row of terraced houses, not far from the town centre and flanked by a small garden at the front and a small yard at the back. Beyond, were cobbled streets and more rows of houses.

For the first few days, Zamir felt very strange and was easily depressed, especially when her husband had gone to work. But after a while she learned to put her fears behind her and decided to explore the territory around her home.

She had already met some of her neighbours and was happy to find that many of them were Pakistani Muslims like herself. They made her welcome in their homes any time. Zamir also found that they had had the same fears when they first came to England and they helped her to adjust her ideas and take advantage of good aspects of the English society.

Soon she realized that there was already a thriving Muslim community in the town and in other parts of industrial England. She felt a kind of security and a sense of belonging in this community where her language, fashion, customs, eating habits and religious traditions were upheld and not regarded as something odd.

As for the children, Shamim was a little disappointed to find that it was quite an old house but it was very cosy and soon she and Bashir were making themselves at home in their bedroom overlooking the back yard. Shamim liked the pink wallpaper. It had lovely white and blue flowers all over it. There was even a small chair. Her father had made one each for them and she would sit on it and then walk to the window to look out exploring the roof-tops and television aerials with her eyes and return to her chair many times before she eventually settled down to her reading or knitting. It was her job to make sure the sheets on the beds were straightened and the quilts pulled back every morning.

The local Asian shops offered the family all their favourite food including tropical fruit, sweetmeats and spices. Abdul regularly visited the butcher, who sold only the specially killed meat which Muslims may eat.

'What are those?' Zamir had enquired of her husband one evening as a pork sausage advertisement appeared on the television screen.

'Pork sausages,' he replied.

'Pork!' she had retorted and immediately switched the picture off, because Muslims must not eat any form of pig meat.

'You'll have to get used to seeing and hearing things you don't like. Just look and listen — but don't taste.' The children had discovered that that was their father's favourite motto.

> What actions are most excellent? To gladden the heart of a human being, to feed the hungry, to help the afflicted, to lighten the sorrow of the sorrowful, and to remove the wrongs of the injured. (*The Hadith*)

The lady next door, Mrs Whitehead, was an elderly widow and Abdul told Zamir to let Shamim do jobs for her. He often wished his wife could speak English so that she could talk to the old lady although they seemed to communicate somehow with gestures and mime. Zamir would help her to hang out the washing and Shamim would bring some groceries for her while Mrs Whitehead sat on the step feeding the pigeons with bread crumbs. Abdul encouraged his family to be kind to the old lady. Had not the Prophet Muhammad stated: 'Paradise lies under the feet of your mother'?

Shamim liked Mrs Whitehead. She decided that since her own grandmother was not around any more and Mrs Whitehead was a very kind lady who gave her sweets and had helped her to make a little vegetable patch at the end of the yard, it was quite in order to look upon her as a new grandmother. She liked looking at the photographs of her children. Father told them they had grown and gone to live far away in the big cities.

6. A village mosque.

'Like uncle Imam-ud-Din?' she had enquired.

'Yes, in a way,' replied her father.

'But why doesn't she go and live with them?' was the innocent reply.

'Oh, some people like to stay on their own,' he told her.

But she was not so sure that Mrs Whitehead did like living alone. She had always been taught that people should not live alone. Mrs Whitehead was always pleased to see her anyway.

'Will real grandmother be coming to live with us soon?' she asked.

'Oh, it is too cold for her. She will come for a holiday when she wants,' her mother told her.

'It is strange not having her to hear my lessons. We learnt a lot together,' she mused as she opened her Arabic reader and began to recite.

The children had begun to attend the local mosque which, unlike the village mosque with its domes and minarets, white walls and courtyard, was a rather bleak looking old terraced house. Zamir helped them to learn their Arabic prayers and passages from the Holy Qur'an, which gave her great pleasure. Her religion was a great strength and comfort to her and she felt that it was too precious a thing to let the blessings which it brought to her slip away under the pressure of modern living. She now felt there was even more need to remind her children of the stories of the great people of Islam and would tell them one every night. She became particularly careful about teaching them to say *Bismillah*, in the name of Allah, before they ate a meal, and thanking God by saying *Alhamdulillah* after the meal. Everyone seemed to be in a hurry. She knew it was her job to make sure that in the bustle and activity of this new life her children should not forget their God.

She was sad to discover that her husband did not say prayers regularly though he attended the communal prayers at lunchtime on the Muslim Holy Day, Friday. Working hours made it almost impossible to keep to the prayer timetable, so his prayer mat remained in the sideboard drawer. However, she had encouraged him to say the late evening prayer every day and the early morning and mid-day prayers at weekends, so that the children might follow their example.

Every morning, before breakfast, Abdul would take down the Holy Qur'an from its high shelf in the cupboard and unwrap its green velvet cover which Zamir had specially made to protect its revered and well-loved pages. The whole family would listen with heads covered and feet bared as Abdul read part of a chapter. Everyone was particularly careful not to turn their backs upon the Holy word, for all Muslims believe that the Qur'an is the final and unchanged word of God as it was revealed to the Prophet Muhammad over 1300 years ago. On such occasions as these, Zamir Akhtar felt peace in her mind.

By the morning hours
And by the night when it is stillest,
Thy Lord hath not forsaken thee. (*The Qur'an* 93:1–3)

SCHOOL DAYS

One day in September was an important day for both Bashir and Shamim. They were to go to school in England for the very first time. Already they had begun to pick up some English words and phrases from Mrs Whitehead and other children in the neighbourhood. They were very excited and also a little anxious about the thoughts of a new school.

7. A Muslim family reading the Holy Qur'an.

The children held their father's hands very tightly as they walked into school. A young teacher, wearing a flowered dress and long blue cardigan greeted them and introduced herself as Miss Clark. Shamim thought she was very pretty and admired her golden hair. Bashir stood looking at the floor while a tear rolled down his cheek and a little lump came into his throat. Miss Clark tousled his hair. 'Ah, Bashir!' she sighed and cuddled him. Then he understood that Miss Clark would be all right. He became aware of children chattering in the classroom nearby. Slowly he undid the zip on his new anorak and made up his mind to join them.

As they entered the room, Miss Clark spoke to the rest of the class and all was quiet. She called to a girl. Shamim noted that she had two plaits instead of one, and they were introduced. It would be Maryam's job to look after Shamim and Bashir until they had settled in. Shamim was glad to be able to talk in her own language but Maryam said that she must try to learn English as quickly as possible as they were not supposed to speak other languages in class.

It was not long before Shamim and Bashir found that they could understand a lot of English, but they found it hard to speak it themselves.

24

8. At school.

Very often they knew what they wanted to say but somehow it didn't sound quite right. 'Her' became 'his', 'She' became 'he', 'v's' were 'b's', 'w's' were 'v's'. 'I stood on the chair' would come out as 'I standed on the chair'. They all had a lot of fun laughing at their mistakes.

Bashir being younger, settled down and found that a lot of the work came out quite naturally. But for Shamim, it wasn't quite as easy. She had been quite clever at school — now she found herself with young children again and many were better than she was. She began to feel left out and pretended that it didn't matter. She liked helping the teacher though and would do little jobs. Maryam proved to be a good friend and helped her as much as she could. Shamim's favourite subject was sums, except the ones with words which she did not understand. She liked adding up and taking away and she knew her tables. She tried to think in English but it slowed her up so much she often gave in and carried on thinking in her own language just as she had done in the village.

Now that the weather was becoming colder, many members of the class preferred not to change for Physical Education activities. Shamim disliked taking her dress off and would not remove her *shalwar*. She had always

25

9. Child in *lehnga*.

been taught that Muslim girls should keep their bodies well-covered. These lessons worried her at first. She refused to take part until her father said it would be all right for her to change into P.E. kit while she was at the junior school.

One of Shamim's favourite lessons was drawing patterns; sometimes her patterns were stuck on the wall, then she would beam with pride. She liked patterns better than pictures. In the village they didn't draw portraits. It was not encouraged in case people once more began to love and admire pictures, people and statues instead of the one God.

One day she had drawn a pattern from her Arabic reader and Miss Clark had asked her about it. She was pleased to tell her that she was learning Arabic 'so that I read good the Holy Qur'an, Miss,' she beamed. 'I'd like to know more about the Holy Qur'an,' Miss Clark had replied and Shamim had brought her readers to school and explained the strange looking squiggles and how the writing ran from right to left and that they had to learn the contents of each reader before they moved on to the next.

An unusual calendar hung on the wall in the staff room. It too, had strange squiggly writing on it. It was a Muslim calendar which Shamim had given to Miss Clark. The Islamic calendar begins from the day the Prophet Muhammad arrived in Medina in 622 C.E. There he received help from his friends. Because the months begin and end with the phases of the moon they make what they call a Lunar Year. Whenever a new moon appears a new month begins. This means that a Muslim year is about ten days shorter than the Christian year which is based upon the movement of the sun. Eventually, each month passes through all the seasons of the year.

Now the Muslim month of *Ramadhan* had arrived. Miss Clark was aware that during this month Muslims were expected to fast, which means going without food and water between dawn and sunset.

Although most of the Muslim children were not fasting because they were too young they hardly ate anything at lunchtime and Miss Clark began to worry in case they grew tired and became ill. Every day she made sure that she spoke for at least ten minutes to every child in the class. It was during one of these conversations with Shamim that she took the opportunity of finding out more about the practice of fasting.

'Are you fasting Shamim?' she had asked.

'No, Miss, only on Friday, our special day of prayer, and at weekends. Daddy says I can try when I am a little older but he says it is too difficult when we are at school.'

'Your mummy and daddy, do they fast?'

'Oh yes, they have breakfast very early, about 4 o'clock, then they do not eat till about 7 o'clock at night.'

'Do they drink water?'

'Oh no, nothing at all while the sun is in the sky. People do not smoke or have parties or go to films.'

Miss Clark nodded. It sounded a very difficult task to her.

'And will it soon be over now?' she enquired.

'Yes, next week, when they see the new moon, then it will be our *Eid.*'

'Will you enjoy that? It is a kind of party, isn't it?'

'Yes, mummy cooks rice and curry and friends come. Then we go to other people's houses and everybody is glad. It is a very happy time.'

'Good. Try to eat a little more dinner if you can won't you?'

'Yes, Miss, but no meat,' they both laughed.

'No meat,' Miss Clark said as she rose and told the children to put their books away. 'Off you go to play.'

A TIME OF CELEBRATION

Shall I tell you the very worst amongst you? Those who eat alone, and whip the servants, and give to nobody. (The Prophet Muhammad)

At the end of the fasting month, the first of *Shawal*, the celebration day, known as *Eid-al-Fitr*, brought crowds of friends and distant relatives to Abdul's house. Zamir spent all morning making spicy meat and potato pastries called *samosas* and gramflour *pakoras* which she fried in deep cooking oil. Shamim watched carefully as her mother lowered the pastries and batter into the hot oil. It spat out furiously and the young girl quickly drew back. Her father had brought lots of sweetmeats from the Sweet Centre in Manchester and these would be distributed to their guests at the end of the day. Shamim and Bashir enjoyed eating the squiggly orange *jalebi* and the carrot pudding the best.

Shamim helped to stir the yoghurt and mix in the salad of tomatoes, onion, cucumber, radish and shreds of fresh crisp lettuce. When the guests arrived, Zamir spent a long time giving out the presents she had brought from friends and relatives. Shamim wondered why some people wept. She was enjoying parading up and down in her brand new pink clothes. Her dress was covered in small silver threaded flowers with a border of large flowers in silver and dark pink thread. Her head was covered by a matching pink shawl bordered with silvery lace. Bashir wore a new blue suit with a jacket that zipped up the front and long trousers. He also had a small red velvet waistcoat bordered with gold braid.

Shamim wanted to know why girls didn't have waistcoats but her father silenced her by presenting her with some velvety slippers covered with silver sequins. They were so delicate and dainty compared to the heavy shoes which the children wore at school. As she looked round at the people sitting on chairs, stools and even curled up on the floor, she remembered those happy family gatherings in the village. It was a regular event there to visit each other's homes. It seemed to her that most people in the village were related in some way, and to her and Bashir all men and women were uncles and aunties.

Mrs Haq, as Zamir was often called now by English people and particularly local officials, usually had to feed large numbers of guests in three sittings. The meal, chicken curry and *chupattis* accompanied by brown fried rice full of mutton chops, was served to the men first while the children sat round the kitchen table. Their glasses were full of orange juice or water. They do not drink any form of alcohol. When their meals were ended Shamim and the various aunties collected up the dishes and washed up. While the tea was being made Shamim took in the fresh fruit and dishes of sweet rice and *churi* made with nuts. She liked to serve because the visitors made a fuss of her and by the end of the evening she was able to pop a pound note or two and various coins into her little money box.

The women ate their meal in the kitchen and gossiped about the children and family matters while the men discussed politics and work. Some of them were talking about plans for a new mosque. Shamim liked to sit and listen for a while. Then she would join the other children playing in the yard or upstairs in the bedroom.

A NEW BORN CHILD

One of her aunties had left her baby in charge of her daughter and Shamim watched eagerly as Zaida changed the nappy and fed her baby brother. He was soft and cuddly with black hair now grown thicker after the first shaving of the head which all Muslim babies undergo. Money amounting to the weight of the shaven hair is then given to the poor.

10. A new mosque still under construction in Manchester.

Shamim still remembered the occasion when Bashir was a new born baby, and her father had whispered the religious words into the tiny ears. The *Adhan* (call to prayer) which she knew well, is whispered into the right ear,

> God is Most Great. God is Most Great. God is Most Great. God is Most Great.
> I bear witness that there is none worthy of being worshipped except God.
> I bear witness that there is none worthy of being worshipped except God.
> I bear witness that Muhammad is the Messenger of God.
> I bear witness that Muhammad is the Messenger of God.
> Come to prayer.
> Come to prayer.
> Come to success.
> Come to success.
> God is Most Great.
> God is Most Great.
> There is no God if not God Himself.

Into the left ear is whispered, the *Iqaamah* which gives the command to rise up to worship. She also knew that at an early age boys were circumcised, and she had read that in Arabia before the time of the Prophet

Muhammad, who taught that all children were part of Allah's creation and therefore precious, baby girls had been buried alive.

Shamim was very glad about this teaching of the prophet and knew that her father was too.

A VISIT TO THE MOSQUE

Miss Clark had been reading books about the religions of the children in her class. She soon discovered there were many more religions than she had thought, but she had never had the opportunity to visit any of their places of worship. Another member of staff was learning an Asian language, *Urdu*, at the Adult Education Centre and had told her about a proposed visit by the *Urdu* class to the Mosque in Horton Street. She had made enquiries and found that it would be quite all right for Miss Clark to join the group.

One evening in November a small group of students including welfare workers, a policeman, the Fire Chief, a railway booking office clerk, several teachers and Miss Clark arrived on the doorstep of the Mosque. *'Assalamu Alaikum* — Peace be with you', greeted the *Imam* and members of the Mosque Committee which is responsible for the management and financial upkeep of the Mosque. *'Wa-alaikum assalam* — and peace be with you,' replied the students. They were led into a hall where they were asked to take off their shoes before they entered a carpeted room with pale green walls decorated only by Arabic writings.

They sat on the floor round the *Imam* who welcomed them and briefly told them about the religion of Islam and the Prophet Muhammad:

'First, I should explain that the religion of Islam which· means complete submission to the Will of Allah was revealed to our Prophet Muhammad, may peace be on him, over a period of 23 years from 609 C.E. and was written down in the Holy Qur'an in the form of *aaya* (verses) and *suras*(chapters). At this time the people of Arabia worshipped idols and behaved like savages rejecting all ideas of one God. Many of the words revealed to the Prophet were acknowledgements of the previous Old Testament Scriptures and Prophets and revealed a very strict code of behaviour in morals, attitude to family, women and children, finance, justice, food and dress habits.'

Belief and the Five Pillars

'Throughout the Prophet's life many of his sayings were written down and are known as *Hadith* or Traditions. Both the Holy Qur'an and the *Hadith* encourage Muslims to be perfect examples to others. Here is a brief list of some of the qualities which Muslims should try to achieve:

> Seek knowledge.
> Be well-mannered, truthful, just, forgiving, tender, humble, and sincere.
> Be gentle in speech, patient, trustworthy and honest.
> Maintain cleanliness by regular washing before and after meals and regular brushing of teeth, having a bath at least once a week and performing ablutions before all prayers.
> Respect the rights of all, including parents, husband, wife, children, relatives, neighbours, poor and weak and be tolerant to non-Muslims.
> Share things willingly, be hospitable to all and lend money without interest.
> Muslims must not commit murder, suicide, adultery, robbery or slander, destroy living creatures and plants without good reasons, drink alcohol, eat pork or unritually killed meat or blood, gamble, take part in lotteries or bet, forge and cheat, take bribes, gossip or be idle, watch crude forms of entertainment or fight amongst themselves.

'The basic beliefs are set out in what are known as the Five Pillars of Islam. The Prophet said, "There are more than 70 departments of the faith and among them the most superior and exalted is belief in the *Kalimah*". This is the first belief that there is no God but Allah and Muhammad is His Prophet.

'The second is the saying of set prayers five times a day at the correct times; dawn, mid-day, afternoon, sunset, late evening. The third is *Zakat*, a small tax on wealth to be given to the poor. Fasting during the month of *Ramadhan* is the fourth and finally the performance of the *Hajj* or pilgrimage to the Holy shrine of the *Ka'aba* in Mecca, if at all possible at least once in a lifetime. A devout Muslim, a person who submits to the will of Allah, will try to do all these things and many other devotions such as *Jihad* which takes different forms; the minor *Jihad* means doing everything possible by thought and deed to further the cause of Islam, the main *Jihad* is against all forms of evil and evil doing; *Zikr* when a person has Allah constantly on his mind; *Tauba* which means repentance of all misdeeds and thoughts. You see, it is not an easy job trying to be the perfect or ideal Muslim!'

Names and Prophets

'Now before I tell you about our Holy Prophet, perhaps you would like to ask me some questions?' Everyone was quiet for a moment then a

11. The Holy Qur'an and its velvet covered box.

young man asked, 'Is Allah the same as the God mentioned in the Bible then?'

'Oh yes,' replied the *Imam*, 'Allah is the name for the one God and we believe he has 99 names including "*Rahman* and *Rahim* — the Compassionate, the Merciful". Muslim names are taken from these names or attributes of God and are usually combined with one of the Prophet's names. We do not use the family or surnames, though in this country some people adopt tribal names and many women add their husband's last name to their own to avoid confusion in the local government offices.'

'That's true — it helps us a lot,' agreed a lady from the Department of Health and Social Security.

'A lot of my Muslim boys have Muhammad as one of their names,' added a teacher. 'It certainly is confusing at first so we call them by the other names.'

'Do you accept the Bible?' the young man continued.

'Yes and no. We do not accept the Bible in its present form because we believe it has been altered too much, but we recognize all the Old Testament prophets, such as Abraham, Noah, Jonah, David, Joseph,

12. The cave called Hira where the Angel Gabriel visited Muhammad.

Moses, also Jesus the son of Mary, may blessings be on them. Perhaps you have noticed some of our people are named after those mentioned in the Bible, Ibrahim (Abraham), Maryam (Mary), Yaqoob (Jacob), Yusuf (Joseph), Isa (Jesus), Saira (Sarah), Yahya (John the Baptist).

'The Holy Qur'an was revealed to Muhammad, may Allah bless him, as the final word of Allah to mankind, for He had sent thousands of Prophets to all nations and tribes before him, but the people had mis-interpreted their word or had failed to believe in Allah at all.'

Muhammad

'Now before the prayers I have just time to tell you a little about the Prophet Muhammad, may Allah bless him. You will have noticed that I pronounce his name with great respect as all Muslims should. So also, we respect the names of all Prophets and the Great Leaders of Islam.

'Muhammad, may Allah bless him, was born in 570 C.E. at Mecca in Saudi Arabia. His father died before his birth and his mother died when he was six. His grandfather looked after him for two years then he also died and the child was looked after by his uncle whom he helped in his work as a merchant. As a young man, he was well-known for his honesty and piety. When he was 25 he married Khadijah, a wealthy widow who had employed him to look after her estate.

'He often used to meditate in the mountains but it was not until he was 40 when he was meditating in a cave called *Hira* that the Angel Gabriel came to him in a vision and told him to proclaim:

Read: In the name of thy Lord Who createth,
Createth man from a clot.
Read: And thy Lord is the most Bounteous,
Who teacheth by the pen,
Teacheth man that which he knew not. (*The Qur'an* 96:1—5)

'At first his followers included only his loving wife, his friend Abu Bakr, his nephew Ali, and Zaid, a slave whom he had freed. As his reputa-tion as *El-Ameen* — the Trusty, went before him, so more people joined his disciples.

'Of course he had many enemies who did their best to get rid of him but I'm happy to say they did not succeed. He died in 632 C.E. at the age of 63.'

'Didn't he have more than one wife?' one lady enquired.

'Oh yes,' the *Imam* smiled, 'while Khadijah was alive, she was his only wife.'

'After her death he did marry other women, most of them widows, who could have been left without means of support. Do not forget that in those days it was not unusual to have lots of wives and they were often treated badly. Islam gave to wives and women respect and rights they had never had before.'

'Who came after Muhammad then?' the lady continued.

'His immediate successors were the elected Rashidin Caliphs Abu Bakr, Umar, Uthman and Ali. They had known the Prophet and were true Muslims of wonderful character who carried on the work of the Prophet wisely and well.'

Miss Clark could see that she was going to be busy in the library during the holidays!

Call to Prayers

Another young man asked, 'You are the *Imam* or leader of the Mosque, could you explain your role, is it that of a priest?'

The *Imam* smiled, stroked his beard and replied, 'We do not have a priesthood in Islam, we owe allegience only to Allah. There are many Muslims who, like myself, have learnt the whole of the Holy Qur'an by heart. This entitles them to be called *Hafiz*. These people are highly respected in the community for as you can imagine it is not an easy task to learn the entire Qur'an in Arabic. Wherever they live, such people usually take over the responsibility of the religious welfare of Muslims and lead the congregation in daily and Friday afternoon prayers. If there is no *Hafiz*, any Muslim could lead the prayers, for all Muslims know from memory the form and the content of the service and parts of the Holy Qur'an. But it is almost time for prayer. In Muslim countries, the *Muezzin* makes the call to prayer from the top of the minaret but here one of our followers makes the call in the corridor. So please cover your heads and turn to face that corner where you see the lectern (*Mehrab*) and the pulpit (*Minbar*) where I stand.

'Now you are facing in the direction of Mecca. You will see that our worship involves many positions of prayer which are in themselves ways of praising Allah. I will leave you now.'

Miss Clark had already noticed that the room was filling up with men, young and old, all wearing *topis* or scull caps. Some wore handkerchieves knotted at each corner. She noticed that prayers began only at a fixed time. She understood this was so that all Muslims could be united in their prayers together even though they were many miles apart.

The prayers consisted of certain Arabic formulas, part taken from the Holy Qur'an and some following the example set by the Prophet. These

36

13. One of the prayer postures.

were all said at the same time by each member of the congregation in standing, kneeling, sitting and prostrating positions. Miss Clark found it fascinating to see everyone moving together and marvelled at the sound of 'popping' made by their lips in the silent prayers as they rapidly mouthed the formulas learnt almost from infancy just as their forefathers and the Prophet Muhammad and his small band of followers had done in the early days of Islam.

When the time of prayers was over, the group had a chance to talk to some of the worshippers who gladly offered information about the uplifting, physically exercising, and relaxing qualities of the prayers.

Some of the women students wanted to know why there were no women present. They received various replies such as, 'women usually pray at home where they are needed to look after and set an example to the children', or 'in purpose-built mosques, women would come and worship but in a separate room, this ensures that thoughts are entirely devoted to Allah'.

Muslim Brothers

Many of the students had noticed that there were no pictures of religious people or the prophets in the room.

'Don't you display pictures of your Prophet?' asked a young lady.

'Oh no, that is not allowed in case we begin to think more of the people in the pictures than God. Nor will you find pictures of the Prophet in any of our books,' replied Mr Khalid, Secretary of the Mosque Committee, 'although next to Allah we love and respect him above all creatures. You will notice many intricate caligraphic patterns, though; this kind of work is developed to perfection in many beautiful world famous mosques.'

'I like the idea of the *Zakat* tax to help the poor. I think that is a very good idea, but what is the true purpose of the pilgrimage?' enquired an elderly lady.

'Ah, the *Hajj* is an event of great enlightenment and joy to all Muslims who experience it. I have been and can assure you I received great benefits from the fortnight I spent there,' replied Mr Khalid. 'It brings together rich and poor, from all nations of the world, with one aim in mind, to acknowledge the greatness of Allah and remember some of the events in the history of the *Ka'aba*. To see everyone regardless of wealth and position wearing the simple white *Ihram*, a dress consisting of two pieces of cloth, walking, talking, eating and worshipping together is a truly wonderful sight.'

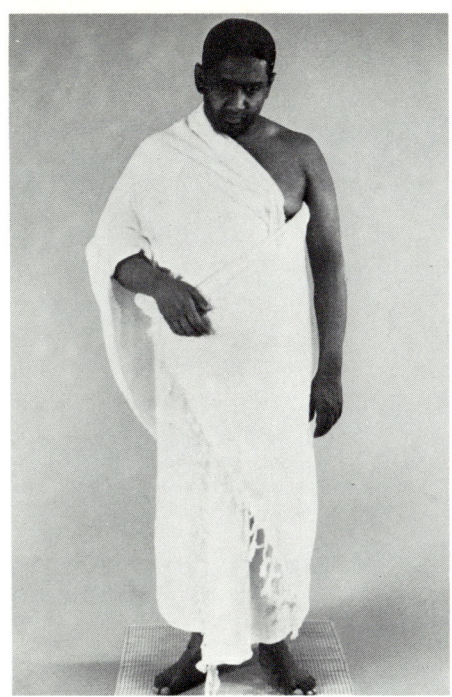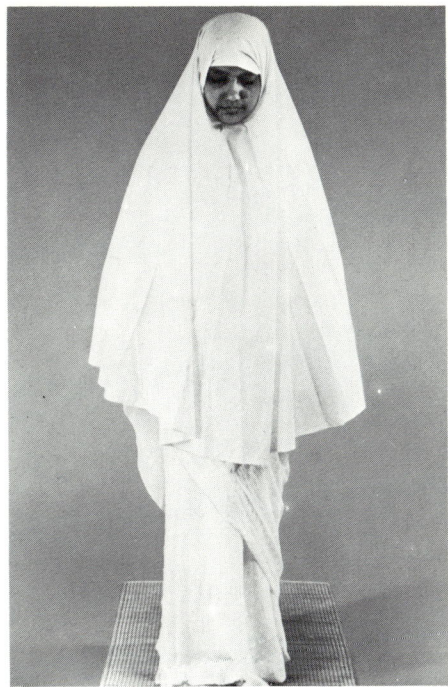

14 & 15. A man and woman wearing the *Ihram*.

As he was talking, the *Imam* began to gather his party. 'We are very limited in our activities here, as this is only a small terrace property,' he said. 'Ideally, all Muslims should be able to congregate here; children should not only come to read and learn but should have rooms in which they can play and talk together. We would like to hold meetings and celebrate our festivals in a grander manner. If you come this way, I will show you where we perform the ablutions, that is washing of hands, face and feet before we say prayers, then you can put your shoes on again and we'll have some tea and cakes . . .'

He continued to chat to the group as he led them into the school room where they were offered English tea and cakes, and looked at a small display of 'Books for Further Information' and those used by children.

Miss Clark noticed some books specially produced for children in English. She flicked through the pages and at the beginning of one she found:

God

There is none like Him,
He has no partners.
He begets not nor is He begotten,
He is Eternal.
He knows everything.
He sees everything.
He is everywhere.
He is the Creator of the Universe.
He is the 'Lord'.
God is Great and Merciful.
He is Kind and Loving.
He has provided us with everything.
He created us in the best form.
He created the world for us.
He sent Prophets to guide us;
To tell us how to obey Him;
How to live like good human beings,
And be happy and successful.
In *Arabic* God is called *Allah*.
Allah is the name for ONE and only ONE GOD.

whilst at the end of another she read:

Hajj is an occasion of great blessings and happiness — to pray in the House of God; to see the *Ka'aba*; to see the Holy places of prophets, and to meet Muslims from all over the world. It is a sort of family reunion; all Muslims, black, white, brown, yellow, meet here as brothers and equal before Allah.

She could not help thinking about all the little faces in the school assembly — there they all were, black, white, brown, and yellow too — all one family praising God.

Then a member of the *Urdu* class made a simple speech both in *Urdu* and English thanking the hosts for the enjoyable and informative evening, and Miss Clark found herself stepping out into the street once more. She thanked the class tutor for letting her join the group.

'I've learnt a lot tonight,' she commented.

'Oh, you are welcome to join the *Urdu* class too,' was the reply.

'Maybe next year,' she laughed.

As she passed the end of Newcombe Street, she looked for a glow of light. The house was in total darkness.

'Gone to sleep,' I expect, she thought to herself, 'God bless you.' And the crescent moon shone brightly in the dark cloudless sky.

THE END OF A TERM

The learned ones are the heirs of the prophets. (*The Hadith*)

One morning during the last term at school before the Christmas holiday, Shamim thought Miss Clark would never notice the little packet on her table. She had carefully wrapped the contents, a small flower shaped brooch and a green silken napkin, in a brown paper bag. The napkin was folded round the brooch. She thought it was the most beautiful napkin she had ever seen. Her mother had *sewn* the words La-ilaha-ilal-lah on it in Arabic script using gold sequins and gold thread. Shamim and Bashir peeped at their teacher from behind their books and waited to see what Miss Clark would do. Shamim was so keen to give Miss Clark the little stone filled brooch which she had bought from the cloth shop with some of the money she had saved from her *Eid* presents that she had not been able to wait until the last day of the term.

Both pairs of eyes lit up as the two children saw Miss Clark pick up the brown paper package. Shamim smiled at the teacher whose puzzled expression when she felt the packet slowly changed to a warm glow of happy surprise as she saw first the green cloth, then the golden needlework and finally the tiny flower glinting and sparkling among the sequins.

'Oh, what a beautiful present!' exclaimed Miss Clark as she held up the brooch and then fastened it to her dress. 'And just look at this children,' she continued as she held up the green cloth glancing in the direction of the now beaming Shamim and Bashir. All the children gasped in wonder at the brilliance of the gold sequinned pattern shining out of the bright green sheen.

'Thank you Shamim and Bashir, it is a beautiful gift. Thank you very much.' Tears began to well up in her eyes and she searched for her handkerchief and blew her nose.

Some of the Muslim children were already putting up their hands saying 'Please, Miss,' all wanting to tell Miss Clark what the gold lettering said.

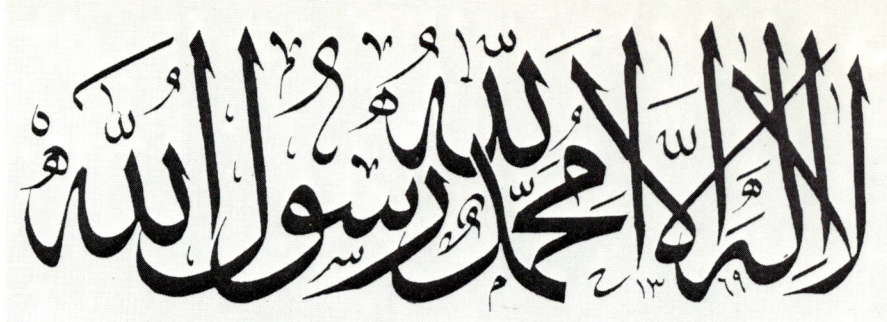

16. Caligraphy – *La-ilaha-ilal-la Muhammad-ur-rasul Allah* or 'There is no god but Allah and Muhammad is His Prophet'.

Of course, Shamim and Bashir knew that Miss Clark could read it for it was the first Arabic word they had taught her.

'What does it say, Shamim?'

Shamim's pale brown complexion reddened slightly, then she said, 'I think teacher can read it best.'

'A good reply,' said Miss Clark grinning, 'I do know what it says children. It says "La-ilaha-ilal-la", which means "there is no God but Allah"'. 'Good,' chorused all the little Muslims who then clapped and cheered with great gusto and everyone else joined in.

Miss Clark waited until they were all quiet again and continued, 'Yes, we are all friends, aren't we? God is our friend too. He is everybody's friend for our Muslim, Hindu, Christian and Sikh children and children of all religions. A short while ago Ragbir was telling us about *Guru Nanak's Birthday*, we held a *Diwali* or Festival of Light service and Maryam and Shamim showed us their new dresses specially made for the end of *Ramadhan*. Now it is time for Christian children to be happy. For they remember the birth of Jesus. Can you remember anything about him?'

Shamim listened with great interest to Miss Clark. She had learnt about Jesus from the stories the *Imam* told them about the prophets in the Holy Qur'an. She had learnt to respect him as a great man of God, but Muslims did not celebrate his birthday as they did that of Muhammad, the Prophet. Soon they would be celebrating the near sacrifice of Ishmael by the Prophet Abraham although Christians believe that the son was Isaac. Maryam had even referred to this *Eid-al-Adha* as their 'Christmas'. But Shamim's mother had said that was not right. In the village, uncle Yusuf usually sacrificed a goat and nearly everyone in the village was invited to a meal or was given lumps of meat to take home. She wondered what

42

they would do in England. Father had told her that his friend would do the same with a sheep or lamb. But she would just have to wait and see.

THE BEGINNING OF A FRIENDSHIP

The best friendship in God's eyes is one who does good to his friends. (*The Hadith*)

On the second day of the Christmas holiday Bashir watched in wonder as the white snow flakes fell outside their bedroom window.

'Oh look, look Shamim,' he cried, beckoning her to come.

Her bed felt snug and warm, as she pushed her nose over the quilt.

'It's cold,' she complained.

'Yes, but it is snowing,' he called.

She whisked the quilt off and jumped out of bed.

'Ugh,' she shuddered, as she caught the full blast of the wintry air. Then as she looked out she gasped, 'Why all the roofs are white and my garden is covered in thick snow! See someone's footprints on the path. They must be the milkman's.' She popped her cardigan on and ran downstairs.

'Isn't it lovely? Isn't it beautiful?' she almost sang as she opened the door and held her hand out to catch some of the falling snow. The tiny crystal flakes melted in the warmth of her hand. 'Oh, look at this mummy,' she begged as she noticed an extra large cluster on the sleeve of her cardigan. 'Isn't Christmas wonderful?'

Her mother looked up sharply, 'Snow has nothing to do with Christmas, snow is snow, and Christmas is Christmas. Now come along. I want to hear you read the Holy Qur'an this morning.' Shamim pulled a face and Zamir's heart sank. Then her daughter turned and ran upstairs. 'All right, mummy,' she called, 'We'll read first, have breakfast, then look at the snow and maybe I will be able to play in it too.'

When Shamim and Bashir went out into the garden they were surprised to see a young girl, about the same age as Shamim, in Mrs Whitehead's garden. She appeared to be rolling a very large snow ball. 'We'll make one of those,' said Shamim as she picked up a lump of snow and packed it together in her gloved hands. As she began to roll the ball in the snow she was amazed to find how quickly the snow collected in a neat stair carpet to increase the size of her once tiny snow ball. Bashir helped her to roll it along.

'Would you like to put it on top of mine?' said a voice. They looked up to see the young girl next door. She had an anorak with the hood pulled over her head so that only a tiny face peeped out.

'There's not enough snow to make his head so could we make it together?'

To make his head? What was she talking about? The two children looked at her, puzzled. The girl smiled and said, 'I am Joanne. Mrs Whitehead is my grandma and I'm staying here for the holiday. I'm making a snowman. See, here is the body — you have made the head.'

Joanne clambered on to the wall and jumped the short drop into their garden. The children watched her in silence as she picked up their large snow ball and signalled them to follow her into her garden. There, she promptly put the second snow ball on top of her own. Shamim and Bashir giggled.

'Now — ah!' she looked round then snapped off some old twigs from a shrub in the corner of the garden and placing them carefully on the small snow ball commented, 'This will do to make eyes — nose — and — a long one for the mouth — there!' she stood back to admire her efforts. Shamim and Bashir stood in wonder, 'A snowman, a snowman,' they shouted.

'Wait a minute,' yelled Joanne as she ran inside.

Soon she returned with a scarf and a pair of old gloves. She wrapped the scarf carefully round the joint where the snow balls met and stuck a glove on either side of his body so that the fingers rested on what now appeared to be his tummy. Shamim, who thought it was great fun had found some more bits of twig and was putting them in a line down the front for buttons.

At that moment Mrs Whitehead appeared at the door. 'Oh, you are clever children. I'm glad you have met. Has your mummy seen it, Shamim?' Shamim ran back to the house and opening the front door called out. Her mother, thinking something was wrong, almost ran down the hall.

'Look at our snowman, isn't he funny?' said Shamim.

'Oh, you did give me a fright,' scolded Zamir, and then she saw the snowman and Mrs Whitehead and a little hooded girl and Bashir holding the snowman's hand.

'Why, that is very clever of you my dears,' she said laughing. 'What a funny little man you have made.'

Shamim was glad to be able to play with Joanne. Her mother didn't like her to wander away from the street and her school friends did not live nearby. Although she could only speak simple English she found she could communicate quite well with English people now. But Joanne was the first English girl she had actually played with, who had accepted her naturally as a friend. At school she played with the girls in her 'Special English Class' and she did not have much chance to meet the English children.

'We had an International Service before the holidays. It was good. There are children of many different religions in our class and we're finding out about them. How old are you?' Joanne asked.

'Eleven,' replied Shamim.

'Oh, I'm twelve. I am at Secondary School now. You'll go there after summer I expect. My grandma says you have not been in England long. Have you got any pictures or magazines I could take to school?'

'We've got some newspapers with some pictures of mosques. I'll ask mummy if you can have them. Would you like to have a look at my readers? I'm sewing a prayer mat.' She was so glad that Joanne wanted her to help her in her school work.

'Brr! It's too cold,' Abdul Haq complained as he entered the front door late that evening, his cloth cap pulled well over his head. 'I see there's a visitor in the garden, next door.'

'Yes, Joanne showed us how to make the snowman, daddy.'

'Joanne?' he raised his eyebrows, puzzled.

'Yes, Mrs Whitehead's grand-daughter. She is staying here for a while and she is my friend, isn't she, mummy? And she is going to come to Mrs Whitehead's every holiday and she lives in London and you have some friends in London and you keep saying you want to visit them . . .'

'Yes, yes, not so fast, my little one,' laughed her father. Both parents looked at each other and smiled.

Shamim had found her first English friend — *and* made her first snowman! Now they really were settling down at last.

There we leave Shamim and her family. No doubt she will have a lot more to tell and discover with her new friend. Like you, they both have a great deal to learn.

We hope that with their friends they will grow up, working and living together in that happiness which comes from true understanding.

O Lord! Lord of my life and of everything in the universe! I affirm that all human beings are brothers unto one another. (*The Hadith*)